Designs by
Ranae Robbins Lee

Published by Provo Craft
Provo, Utah
Managing Editor, Clella Gustin
Design and Book Coordinator,
Barbara Sanderson
Photography by Craig Young

DEDICATION: This book is dedicated to all those wonderful people out there, who spend their time truly being "Heaven's Helpers" quietly showing unselfish acts of kindness to those around them and rarely being noticed for it. May God bless all those whose positive attitudes and love make us feel we've experienced a little bit of Heaven on Earth!

ACKNOWLEDGEMENTS: A very special thanks to God who has truly blessed my life. To my family, John, Jennifer, Andrew, Ryan, Becca, Stephen, Jess, Manda, and Jared for all their patience, love and support. To Kay Banks, for her help and humor. To my dear Mother, Ina Robbins, for her never ending support, wisdom and example. To the great people at Provo Craft, Clella Gustin, Barbara Sanderson, Robert, Craig and Jo and all the others working behind the scenes who helped make this dream possible. May God bless you all!

For your convenience, Provo Craft computer numbers have been listed. Wholesale orders my be placed at the Provo Craft Warehouse, 1-800-937-7686, 285 East 900 South, Provo, Utah 84606. If you do not have a wholesale account, you may order retail from the Provo Craft Shipping Department at 1-800-563-8679, 295 West Center Street, Provo, Utah 84601.

Alternate wood sources for wood not cut by Provo Craft are:
A & P Crafts Supply, 1-800-748-5090, 850 West 200 South, Lindon, Utah 84042, and Hansens' Wood Crafts 1-801-227-7189, 460 East 1070 South, Orem, Utah 84097.

Copyright© Ranae Robbins Lee February 1998. All rights reserved under the Pan American and International Copyright Conventions. Photocopying and all other types of mechanical reproduction are prohibited. The patterns in this book may be hand painted for fun and personal profit. No design in this book may be reproduced for mass marketing such as the gift industry or transmitted in any form or by any information storage and retrieval system without permission from the designer.
ISBN 1-58050-028-5

Provo Craft will make every effort to maintain an inventory of those wood items shown in our books; however, we cannot guarantee that they will be available for the sales life of the book.

Table Of Contents:

"Tweet Or Not To Eat"	5
Key-Purr Of The Birds	7
Purr-Fect Kitty	8
Kindness Garden	10
Lunch Time Cuckoo Clock	12
Cat Heaven	13
Come And Get It	15
Plant A Kiss	16
A Stitch In Time Saves 9 Lives	17
Don't Hide Your Lite	18
Mom's Halo	22
Endure To The End	23
Sunshine Quilt	25
Guardian Kitty (Plant Stake)	26

GENERAL INSTRUCTIONS:

Wood Cutting: Trace each project onto the wood (avoiding knots). Then cut out each specified piece. The lamp in this book requires precision cutting. Use a good straight wood that is free of warps.

Wood Preparations: A palm sander is a good investment. There are many good brands on the market, just be sure replacement parts and sand paper are readily available. Sand the wood well. Then use a tack cloth to remove all dust. Seal the wood with your favorite sealer. I prefer Designs From the Heart or McCloskey's Wood Sealer. Sealing the wood properly is essential to good success. On unsealed wood, the paint grabs too quickly, moisture raises the wood grain leaving an uneven painting surface, and lining pens smudge and bleed. So please remember this most important step before beginning to paint. After sealing, sand one last time with a 220 fine grit sandpaper.

Tracing: Trace the pattern onto tracing paper (see through), then place graphite paper (shiny side down) between the pattern and the project making sure the pattern is secure. Trace over the pattern using a stylus or pencil. (Trace only the basic patterns, add the details later as needed.)

Basecoat: Apply 2 to 3 thin layers of paint to fill in the basic color.
Floating: Dampen the brush in clean water, blot lightly on the paper towel, then load one corner of the brush with paint, blend the paint by stroking the brush back and forth on the palette till the paint and water blend to achieve a faded look then apply to the project. The side with the paint should look deep and then slowly fade to nothing on the water side of the brush.
Stipple: I prefer Loew Cornell fabric dye brushes for the stippling. Dip a dry brush in the paint, then blot on a paper towel until most of the paint is out of the brush then apply with a bouncing motion to project. Apply several thin layers for best results. Clean and dry the brush well before changing colors or old paint can get trapped in the brush and end up ruining a project.
Highlight and Shade: Float or stipple the area to deepen the contrast and add dimension.
Lining: I prefer using Itoya .1, .3 and .5 permanent lining pens. Micron Pigma pens also work well. (Refer to the pattern for details.) Line only a dry surface or pens can clog. If this happens brush the pen tip lightly across very fine sandpaper to clear the clog. Use a light touch so you don't ruin the pen's tip.
Paints: I've used Deco Art Americana and Delta Ceramcoat in this book. If you can't find the color you need in the brand stated ask your local paint supplier if they carry color comparison charts, so you can substitute a similar color in a different brand. All paint used in this book is waterbased acrylic.
Dots: Dots can be made by using a stylus or wood end of a paintbrush. For large dots I used the wood end on a stipple or stencil brush. Dip in paint for each dot you make to achieve a uniform look. Descending dots are made by dipping once then making several dots in a row, without redipping again.
Finish: I prefer Krylon Matte Spray 1311 for all spray sealing. Use several thin coats, letting it dry between each layer. Spraying too heavily may cause linework to bleed or smudge.
Gluing: I've used Elmer's wood glue or titebond wood glue for the projects in this book. On some projects, gluing is needed before painting. Please follow the project instructions for the best results. After painting, assemble and glue the projects before applying a final finish, otherwise the project tends to be weaker and glue doesn't bond well. Glue guns are used mainly for fabric.
Fabric: On many projects in this book I've used some very simple sewing techniques. All fabric has been torn not cut to the needed size.
Gather: Thread the needle, tie a knot in one end of the thread. Insert the needle in the cloth. Stitch in and out in a straight line to the edge of the cloth. Push the cloth along the thread till it bunches up near the end of the knot. Adjust the gathers in the fabric to fit to the length needed then tie a knot in the thread to hold the gathers in place. See illustration.

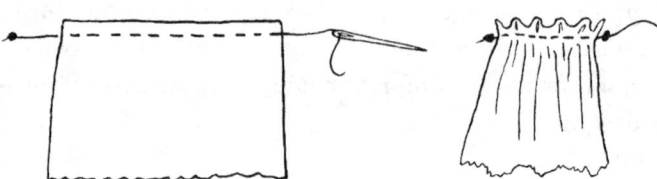

Brushes: I prefer Loew Cornell Brushes on all projects:
Shading: #2, #6 and #10,   *Lining:* 10/0,   *Stippling:* #6 Fabric dye brush

Note: On some of the projects in this book, first sealing is done after the project is pre-assembled and glued. This is necessary to make sure the project is solid and won't come apart. Please follow all pre-assembly instructions as given.

"TWEET OR NOT TO EAT" 11-2175

PALETTE:

DELTA CERAMCOAT
- Ivory
- Black
- Kim Gold (Gleams)
- Maple Sugar Tan
- White
- Barn Red
- Medium Flesh

DECOART AMERICANA
- Salem Blue
- Berry Red
- Primary Yellow
- Victorian Blue
- Ultra Blue Deep
- Shading Flesh
- Baby Blue
- Light Cinnamon

SUPPLIES:
- Stylus
- Itoya .1 and .3 Lining Pens
- (1) Small Wood Heart (for wing)
- 10/0 Liner Brush
- #6 Fabric Dye Brush (for stippling)
- Wood Glue
- Krylon Matte Spray 1311
- Checkerboards Stencil #41-0530
- Grey Graphite Paper (for tracing pattern)
- #2 Shader Brush
- #6 Shader Brush

WOODCUTTING HINTS: The cat is cut from 3/4" wood. The round circle back is cut from 3/4" wood and is 3-1/2" across (a 3-1/2" circle is illustrated on page 11). The cat hand with the bird is cut from 1/2" wood. The finished size is 6" x 8".

PAINTING INSTRUCTIONS:

1. Using grey graphite paper, trace the basic pattern on the wood, leaving out the details.
2. **Ivory:** Paint the cat's face, tail and both hands.
3. **Salem Blue:** Paint the bird.
4. **Victorian Blue:** Paint the cat's overalls. Shade the bird. Paint the small wood heart.
5. **Salem Blue:** With a lining brush, paint the lines on the small wood heart. Using a stylus, dot each point where the lines cross.
6. **Baby Blue:** Paint the pocket on the cat. Stipple the highlights on the cat's tummy.
7. **Maple Sugar Tan:** Paint the cookie.
8. **Berry Red:** Paint the cat's sleeve.
9. **Barn Red:** Using the medium Checkerboards Stencil, stencil checks on the cat's sleeve.
10. **Ultra Blue Deep:** Using a liner brush, paint plaid lines on the cat's sleeve.
11. **White:** Paint the cat's wings and shoes. With a fine liner brush fill in the narrow double lines on the cat's plaid sleeve, next to the dark blue lines. Fill in the eyes on the bird. Stipple highlights on the bird's head and tummy.
12. **Light Cinnamon:** Using the wood end of the brush, dot the chips on the cookie.
13. **Kim Gold:** Paint the halo on the cat. Line the criss-crosses on the cat's wings. Paint the edges on the wings.
14. **Medium Flesh:** Fill in the cat's nose.
15. **Itoya .3 Pen:** Fill in the letters on the cat's pocket, "Tweet or Not to Eat".
16. **Black:** Using a stylus, dot the words on the cat's pocket. Fill in the dark area behind the bird's feet. Dot the cat's and bird's eyes and cat's fingernails. Stipple the spots on the cat's face, both hands and tail.
17. **Primary Yellow:** Paint the bird's beak and toes. Fill in paw tracks on the bottom of the cat's shoes.
18. **Shading Flesh:** Stipple the blush on the cat's cheeks. Fill in the cat's ears. Float shade on the paw tracks on the bottom of the shoes.
19. **White:** Add a comma stroke and dots to highlight the cat's halo.
20. **Itoya .1 Pen:** Line and stitch everything (refer to the pattern).
21. Using wood glue, glue the small wood heart on the bird, glue the hand with the bird onto the cat. Glue the 3-1/2" round circle on the back of the cat.
22. **Spray Seal:** Using Krylon Matte Spray 1311, seal the entire lid. (Use several thin coats. Let dry between each coat.)

(Pattern is on page 6)

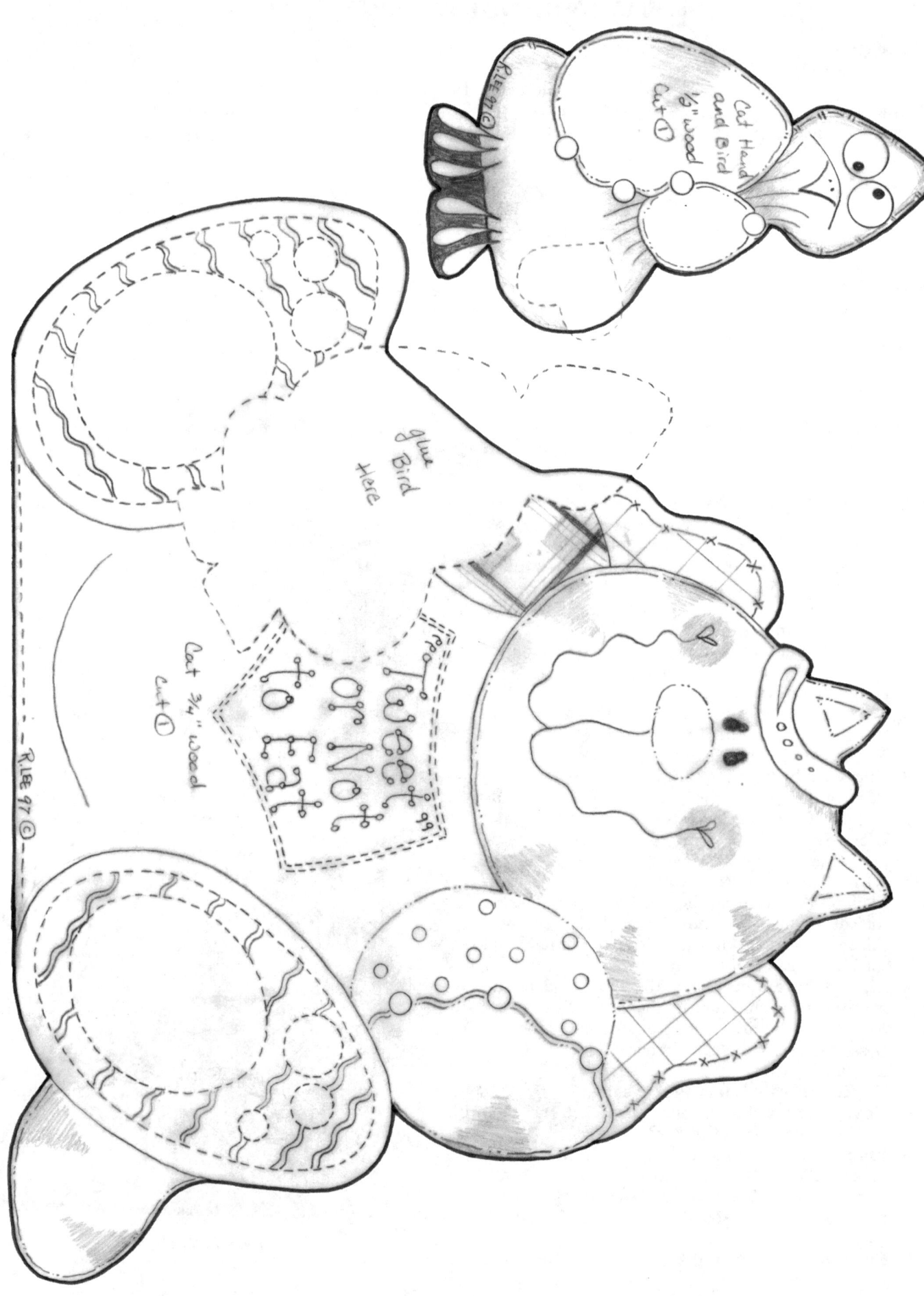

KEY-PURR OF THE BIRDS 11-2176

PALETTE:

DELTA CERAMCOAT
Dolphin Grey
White
Maple Sugar Tan
Dusty Mauve
Black
Kim Gold (Gleams)

DECOART AMERICANA
Sand
Napa Red

SUPPLIES:

Tooth Brush
(2) 1-1/2" Wooden Eggs
(2) 1/2" Cup Hooks
Needle and Thread
Red Fabric Torn 8" x 3-1/2"
Krylon Matte Spray 1311
Wood Glue
Itoya .5 Pen #6 Shader
10/0 Liner Brush
Stylus
(2) 3/8" Screw Eyes
(2) Key Rings
Fabric for 2 Small Patches 3/8" x 3/8"
Tan Fabric Torn 3-1/2" x 2-1/2"
Glue Gun
Saw Tooth Hanger
#6 Fabric Dye Brush
Graphite Paper (for tracing the pattern)

WOODCUTTING HINTS: The cat is cut from 3/4" wood. The wings and birdhouse piece are cut from 1/2" wood.

WOOD PREPARATION: The wooden eggs may need to be pre-drilled for the screw eyes to go in. The overall finished size is 13" x 6".

PAINTING INSTRUCTIONS:
1. **Sand:** Paint the cat's, face, legs, hands and one of the wooden eggs.
2. **Dolphin Grey:** Paint the birdhouse. Using a tooth brush spatter the sand colored egg.
3. **White:** Paint the cat's bloomers and the wings.
4. **Maple Sugar Tan:** Stipple the spots on the cat's hands, legs and face. Paint the other wooden egg.
5. **Napa Red:** Paint the roof of the birdhouse. Using a toothbrush spatter the tan egg.
6. Trace the pattern onto the cat's face, legs, wings and the birdhouse.
7. **Dusty Mauve:** Stipple the blush on the cat's cheeks. Dot the cat's nose and fill in the ears.
8. **Kim Gold:** Paint the cat's halo. Line the wings and paint the edges of the wings.
9. **Itoya .5 Pen:** Line everything (refer to the pattern). Apply the lettering on the birdhouse ("Key-Purr of the Birds"). Apply the lettering on the cat's wings, ("Watch over all... Both large and small") and ("A kitty's work... is Never Done").
10. **Black:** Dot the cat's eyes and paint the shoes. Fill in the hole on the birdhouse. Dot all the lettering.
11. **White:** Paint the highlights on the cat's halo. Using a small lining brush make one small comma stroke, followed by three graduated dots.
12. **Wood Glue:** Glue two small 3/8" x 3/8" fabric patches on the front of the birdhouse under the lettering. Glue the wings on the back of the cat.
13. **Assemble:** Screw the cup hooks into the birdhouse and screw eyes into the tops of the eggs. Attach the key rings to the screw eyes and hammer the sawtooth hanger onto the back of the Key-Purr of the Birds. Using a needle and thread make a running stitch along one 8" side of the red fabric (to make the cat's dress). Adjust the gathers to fit at the cat's neck. Gather one 3-1/2" side of the tan fabric (to make the apron) and adjust as needed. Next center the apron over the dress, with gathers along the top edge together. Using a glue gun, glue both onto the cat at the cat's neck. Then center the birdhouse just below the cat's nose and glue in place over the fabric.
14. **Sealer:** Using Krylon Matte Spray 1311, lift the dress and seal all the pieces, including the eggs.

PURR-FECT KITTY 11-2177

PALETTE:

DELTA CERAMCOAT
Dolphin Grey   Liberty Blue   Maple Sugar Tan
Barn Red   Dusty Mauve   Black
Kim Gold (Gleams)

DECOART AMERICANA
Titanium Snow White   Sand
Light Buttermilk   Cadmium Yellow

SUPPLIES:
Krylon Matte Spray 1311
(4) Small Screw Eyes
Itoya .5 Pen
(2) 4" Pieces Jute
(2) 1" Wooden Hearts
Wood Glue
#10 Shader
Green Fabric Torn 24" x 10-1/2" (for dress)
Green Fabric 1/2" Wide approximately 45" long
#6 Fabric Dye Brush (for stippling)
(1) White 4" Round Pineapple Doily (collar)

19 Gauge Wire
Glue Gun
2 Ply Jute 45" long
Graphite Paper
Needle and Thread
10/0 Liner Brush
Red Fabric 8" x 1/2"
Tan Fabric 8" x 7-1/2" (apron)

WOODCUTTING HINTS: The cat, two legs and spacer are all cut from 3/4" wood. The wings and arms are cut from 3/8" wood. The over all finished size is 20" x 7".

WOOD PREPARATION: Before painting, using wood glue, glue the spacer on the lower front of the cat's body.

PAINTING INSTRUCTIONS:
1. **Dolphin Grey:** Paint the two small wood hearts (set aside).
2. **Titanium White:** Paint the wings.
3. **Sand:** Paint the cat and spacer and both sides of the legs.
4. **Barn Red:** Paint the cat's sleeves.
5. **Liberty Blue:** Paint the bird (on the nest). Line the two small wood hearts.
6. **Light Buttermilk:** Paint the cat's bloomers.
7. **Cadmium Yellow:** Paint the bird's beak.
8. **Maple Sugar Tan:** Stipple stripes on the cat's face and legs. Dot the sleeves.
9. Trace the pattern on the cat's face.
10. **Dusty Mauve:** Stipple the cheeks on the cat. Dot the nose and fill in the ears.
11. **Kim Gold:** Stipple shade on the edges of the wings. Line the wings. Fill in the halo.
12. **Itoya .5:** Fill in all the lettering on the cat's wings ("Charity Never Faileth", "XOX Bear in Mind...You Must Bee Kind XOX", "Love One Another"..."Kindness is Heavens Way of Saying I Love U"). Line the remainder of the cat (refer to the pattern).
13. **Black:** Fill in both sides of the cat's shoes. Dot the lettering and the cat's and bird's eyes.
14. Glue the wings on the back of the cat (avoiding the drill holes for the arms). Glue the wooden hearts on the bird sideways for wings.
15. Using Krylon Matte Spray 1311, spray the entire project.
16. **Fabric:** With dark green fabric, tear the fabric to measure 24" x 10" (for dress). Gather one long edge of the fabric with a needle and thread and adjust to fit the cat's neck (front and sides only). Using the same fabric, tear a piece that is 45" x 1/2" (for nest). With the tan fabric, tear a piece that is 8" x 7-1/2" and gather one shortside with a needle and thread for the cat's apron. Using red fabric tear a piece 8" x 1/2" and tie into a bow. Cut a 4" pineapple doily in half for the collar.
17. **Gluing:** Using a glue gun, glue the jute and green fabric strips in loops for the bird nest. Glue the dress, apron and doily in place. (Tuck the doily under at the neck to cover the cut edges.) Glue the bow on the doily.
18. Wire the arms onto the cat over the dress. Curl the wire and smash at the top of the sleeve to secure the arms in place. You will need to poke the wire from the back to the front through the drill holes in the cat, then through the dress and arms.
19. **Assemble:** Attach one screw eye to the top of each leg. Attach two screw eyes to the front of the spacer. Tie the legs to the body with 4" pieces of jute, leaving approximately 1" between the body and legs. Glue the wings in place.

KINDNESS GARDEN   11-2178

PALETTE:

DELTA CERAMCOAT

White	Dolphin Grey	Maple Sugar Tan	Autumn Brown
Dusty Mauve	Black	Kim Gold (Gleam)	

DECOART AMERICANA

Sand	Napa Red	Victorian Blue	Cadmium Yellow
Cadmium Orange	Mint Julep Green	Leaf Green	Hauser Dark Green
Bright Green	Olive Green	Peaches and Cream	

SUPPLIES:

One Clay Watering Can	1-3/8" Wood Flower Pot	(1) 3/4" Wood Heart
3/16" Dowels	Wood Glue	19 Gauge Black Wire
Itoya .3 and .5 Pens	10/0 Liner	Glue Gun
Thin Jute	Needle and thread	#6 Shader
Needle and thread	Graphite Paper	
Sweethearts Stencil #41-0527	Fabric Scraps (to tie on signs)	
Tan Fabric 2" x 3" (for apron)	Green Fabric 1/2" x 7" (for bow)	
Red Fabric 15" x 3-1/2" (for dress)	#6 Fabric Dye Brush (for stippling)	
(3) Novelty Pipe Cleaner Bumble Bees		

WOOD PREPARATION: Note: When preparing wood, avoid sealing areas that will be glued later. Final spray seal only after all the pieces are glued in place, otherwise the individual pieces don't glue well to sealed surfaces. Glue all the dowels into the signs and birdhouse, before painting. Do not glue the dowels into the base yet.

WOODCUTTING HINTS: The cat and cat shoes are cut from 3/4" wood. The pea bush, pea sign, care-ots sign, care-ots, birdhouse, beehive, cat's arm and wings are cut from 3/8" wood. The base is 3-1/2" x 10" cut from 1-1/2" wood. The dowels are cut 4" long for the sweet peas sign and 3-1/4" for the care-ot sign. The birdhouse dowel is 5-1/4" long. The overall finished size is 9-1/2" x 10" x 3-1/2".

PAINTING INSTRUCTIONS:

1. **White:** Paint the edges of the base, both signs, cat's wings and bloomers.
2. **Sand:** Paint the cat's face, both hands and legs. Using the Sweethearts Stencil, stencil medium hearts around the edges of the base.
3. **Dolphin Grey:** Paint the birdhouse and 3/4" wooden heart.
4. **Maple Sugar Tan:** Stipple the spots on the cat legs, arms and face. Paint the bottom of the flower pot.
5. **Napa Red:** Paint the roof and dowel on the birdhouse and the top of the flower pot.
6. **Victorian Blue:** Paint the bird. Line the small wooden heart. Paint the dowel on the sweet peas sign and the heart on the clay watering can.
7. **Cadmium Yellow:** Paint the beehive, beak on the bird and the dowel on the care-ots sign.
8. **Cadmium Orange:** Paint the care-ots.
9. **Autumn Brown:** Paint the top of the base. Lightly stipple the shades on the edges of the beehive.
10. Using graphite paper, trace the pattern on the cat's face.
11. **Dusty Mauve:** Stipple the cat's cheeks. Fill in the ears. Dot the cat's nose.
12. **Leaf Green:** Paint the pea bush.
13. **Hauser Dark Green:** Stipple the shades on the pea bush. Paint the cat's sleeves.
14. **Bright Green:** Paint the care-ot tops and pea pods.
15. **Leaf Green:** Float shade on the sides of the care-ot tops.
16. **Olive Green:** Dot the peas on the pea pods.
17. **Peaches and Cream:** Lightly stipple the highlights on the care-ots.
18. **Mint Julep Green:** Stipple the highlights on the care-ot tops and pea bush.
19. **Kim Gold:** Paint the edges on the cat's wings and the halo. Line the cat's wings.
20. **Sand:** Dot the cat's sleeves.
21. Trace the words onto the cat's wings, the base and the signs.
22. **Itoya .5 Pen:** Write all the words on the base ("A Garden Filled with Kindness Brings a Harvest Full of Love!"). With a .3 pen write the words on the cat's wings ("Bee Sweet") and ("Plant a Kiss..and Watch Love Grow"). Write the words on the signs and line and stitch everything else. Refer to the pattern.
23. **Black:** Paint the cat's shoes, the space between the care-ots, and the heart on the beehive. Dot the hole on the birdhouse. Dot the cat's and bird's eyes. Dot all the lettering.
24. **Assemble:** Using red fabric cut a 1-1/2" notch out of the top left corner of the fabric (see illustration).

Using a needle and thread gather the top edges to fit around the front, sides and back of the cat's neck. The notch goes under the cat's extended right arm. Glue in place with a glue gun. Using a needle and thread gather the one short edge of the tan fabric (for the apron) and glue in place at the top of the cat's dress. Cut a 3" piece of 19 gauge wire, curl and smash the end of the wire then poke the uncurled end through the back of the wings, back of the cat's dress and the hole in the back of the cat, then through front of the cat's dress and back of the arm. Secure the wire by curling and smashing it again in front of the cat's shoulder. With the green fabric tie a fabric bow and glue onto the cat's neck. Tie the watering can to the hole in the cat's left hand with jute. Curl the bumble bee wires on a pencil or paint brush. Glue one bee to the back of the care-ot sign and two bees to the beehive.

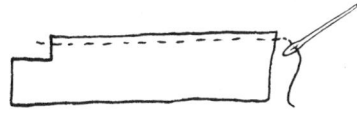

25. **Wood Glue:** Glue the sweet pea sign and dowel on the left back side of the base. Glue the shoe on the cat and the cat on the base center back. Glue the wooden heart on the bird for the wing, the pea bush in front of the sweet pea sign. Then glue the hive in the front of the bush and the cat's foot. Glue the flower pot in front of the cat's other toe, the birdhouse and dowel in the hole on the back right side of the base, the care-ot sign in front of the birdhouse and the care-ots at the front right side of the base. Tie scraps of fabric under both signs.
26. **Spray Sealer:** Seal all of the project with Krylon Matte Spray 1311.

*Circle back for
"Tweet Or Not To Eat"
on page 5*

LUNCH TIME CUCKOO CLOCK

This wood is not available through Provo Craft.

PALETTE:

DELTA CERAMCOAT			DECOART AMERICANA		
White	Ivory	Barn Red	Cadmium Yellow	Victorian Blue	BabyBlue
Silver (Gleams)	Jubilee Green	Black	Ultra Blue Deep	Pumpkin	Calico Red
Medium Flesh	Kim Gold (Gleams)		Shading Flesh		

SUPPLIES:

- (2) 1/4" Screw Eyes
- (2) 36" Beaded Chain Extensions
- 1/2" Small Wood Heart
- Wood Glue
- Graphite Paper
- (2) 3/8" Screw Eyes
- (1) 1" x 1-5/16" Wooden Half Robin's Egg
- Checkerboards Stencil #41-0530
- One 3-1/2" Clock Fitup
- Krylon Matte Spray 1311
- Glue Gun
- Saw Tooth Hanger
- Stylus
- Itoya .3 Lining Pen

Two Medium Size Pine Cones (Pre drill the tops of the pine cones for the chains)
#6 Fabric Brush, #2, #6, and #10 Shaders, 10/0 Liner

WOODCUTTING HINTS: The main clock board, cat and lower board are all cut from 3/4" wood. The cat's arms with scissors, window box and two roof pieces are all cut from 1/4" wood. The overall finished size is 18-1/2" x 9".

WOOD PREPARATION: The two roof pieces are sanded to a 40° angle at the top. Glue the lower board in place before staining. Using Deco Art Walnut Gel Stain, stain everything except the cat, then prepare all the pieces by sealing with Designs From the Heart before painting.

PAINTING INSTRUCTIONS:

1. Trace the basic patterns onto the wood using graphite paper.
2. **White:** Paint the cat's wings and the soles and toes of the shoes.
3. **Ivory:** Paint the cat's face and hands.
4. **Calico Red:** Paint the cat's sleeves and tongue. Then paint the large flowers on the clock, window box and lower board.
5. **Barn Red:** Using the Checkerboards Stencil, apply 3/8" checks on the cat's sleeves. Using a #2 shader brush, float along the inside petals on the red flowers and float along the bottom of the red flower on the window box.
6. **Victorian Blue:** Paint the cat's overalls, side flowers on the window box and upper flowers on the clock board. Also paint the two middle comma strokes on the lower board. Base the bird (half egg).
7. **Baby Blue:** Paint the cat's cuffs and pocket on the overalls, the centers on the side flowers on the window box, and comma stroke on the blue flowers on the clock board and lower board. Paint the small wood heart.
8. **Ultra Blue Deep:** Float shade on the cuffs of the pants. Paint plaid lines on the cat's sleeves. Then dot the small wood heart.
9. **Silver (Gleams):** Paint the blades on the scissors.
10. **Pumpkin:** Paint the handles on the scissors.
11. **Cadmium Yellow:** Paint the beak on the bird. Fill in the paw prints on the bottom of the cat's gym shoes.
12. **Jubilee Green:** Using a small liner brush, dip the brush in green, turn over and dip the brush in yellow (double load) then paint all the leaves.
13. **Kim Gold:** Paint the cat's halo. Line and edge the cat's wings.
14. **White:** Make all dots on and near the flowers. Some are graduated dots (made by dipping the wood end of a brush into the paint one time to make all the dots consecutively without redipping). Paint a comma stroke and dots on the halo to highlight. Using a #2 shader, float highlights on all the red flowers along the top edges of the flowers and petals, then with a liner brush paint fine double white lines on the cat's sleeves. Dot the bird's eyes and paint the cat's sharp teeth.
15. **Shading Flesh:** Float shade on the cat's paw prints on the shoes. Fill in the cat's ears. Stipple the cat's cheeks.
16. **Medium Flesh:** Paint the cat's nose.
17. **Black:** Stipple the spots on the cat's face and hands. Paint the tops of the shoes. Dot the cat and bird eyes and the beak. Base the negative spaces in the scissors handles and the hole for the bird.
18. **Lining Pen:** Using an Itoya .3 lining pen, refer to the pattern and line and stitch everything. Outline all the flowers and dots, the bird's eyes and the bird's beak.
19. **White:** Fill in the shoe laces on the cat's shoes.

20. **Assemble:** Attach the sawtooth hanger to the top center on the back of the clock board. Then using wood glue, glue the roof in place (angled edges matching), glue the arms on the cat and the cat on the roof. Glue the window box in place. Glue the half egg over the window box (so the bird is sitting in the doorway). Then glue the small wood heart onto the bird for the wing. Next put all the screw eyes in the back of the lower board with two small ones in the middle and two large on the outer edges, all approximately 1-1/2" apart. Thread the two beaded chain extensions through the screw eyes so you end up with four chains hanging down. Using a glue gun, glue the outside chain ends into pre-drilled pine cones.
21. Using Krylon Matte spray 1311 seal all the wood and let it dry. Then insert the clock fitup according to the packaging instructions.

CAT HEAVEN

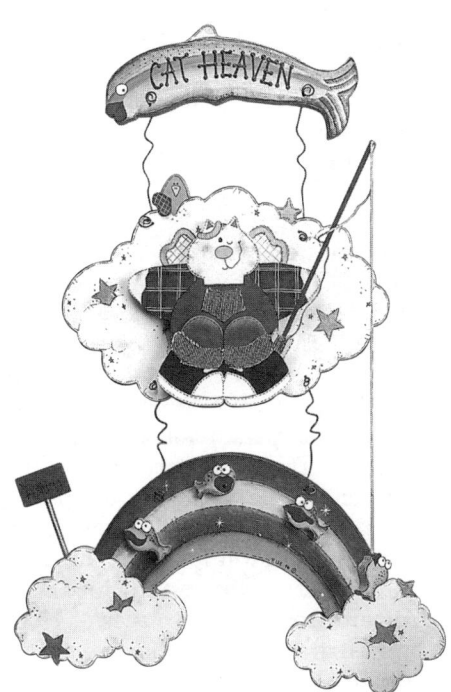

This wood is not available through Provo Craft.

PALETTE:
DECOART AMERICANA

Buttermilk	Berry Red	Victorian Blue
Indian Turquoise	Baby Blue	Orchid
Taffy Cream	Salem Blue	Hauser Dark Green
Shading Flesh	Cadmium Yellow	True Blue
Cadmium Orange		

DELTA CERAMCOAT

White	Tompte Red	Silver (Gleams)
Emerald Green	Pumpkin	Medium Flesh
Maple Sugar Tan	Barn Red	Jubilee Green
Black		
Kim Gold (Gleams)		

SUPPLIES:

19 Gauge Black Wire	Itoya Lining Pen	Saw Tooth Hanger	Denim Fabric Scraps
1/2" Wood Heart	17" of Blue Embroidery Floss	Glue Gun	Wood Glue
Stylus	Krylon Matte Spray 1311	Checkerboards Stencil #41-0530	

#6 Fabric Dye Brush (for stippling), 10/0 Liner Brush, and #2 and #6 Shader
(2) 1/8" Dowels Cut 2-1/4" long for (no fishing sign) and 6" long (fishing pole)

WOODCUTTING HINTS: The rainbow, cloud and large fish are cut from 3/4" wood. The cat is cut from 1/2" wood. The cat's legs, four small fish and small sign are cut from 3/8" wood. The overall finished size is 18" x 12".

PAINTING INSTRUCTIONS:
1. **White:** Paint all the clouds including cat's wings and toes and soles on the cat's shoes.
2. **Buttermilk:** Paint the cat's face, hands and tail on the cloud.
3. **Berry Red:** Paint the top stripe on the rainbow and the cat's sleeves.
4. **Victorian Blue:** Paint the cat's overalls (both pieces), body and knees. Paint the small wood heart.
5. **Silver (Gleams):** Paint four small fish and the large fish sign.
6. **Jubilee Green:** Paint the third stripe down on the rainbow.
7. **Indian Turquoise:** Paint the bottom stripe down on the rainbow.
8. **Baby Blue:** Stipple shade here and there on the clouds.
9. **Orchid:** Stipple shade on the clouds (clean out brush well).
10. **Taffy Cream:** Stipple highlights on the clouds.
11. **Salem Blue:** Paint the small bird sitting on the cloud. Stipple highlights on the cat's knees. Paint fine plaid lines on the small wooden heart.
12. **Barn Red:** Using the Checkerboards Stencil, apply 1/4" checks on the cat's sleeves.
13. **Hauser Dark Green:** Using a #6 shader, float shade on the top and bottom of all the fish, shade the tail on the large fish, then with a liner brush paint plaid lines on the cat's sleeves.
14. **Shading Flesh:** Float the center stripe on all the fish. Fill in the cat's ears. Stipple blush on the cat's cheeks.
15. **Cadmium Yellow:** Paint the bird's beak and second stripe on the rainbow. Then float the last stripe on all the fish (next to the Shading Flesh color). Float highlights on the top of the green stripe on the rainbow.
16. **Maple Sugar Tan:** Paint the fishing reel.
17. **Cadmium Orange:** Highlight the bottom of the red rainbow stripe.
18. **Emerald Green:** Float shade on the top of the blue rainbow stripe and the bottom of the green rain bow stripe.
19. **Pumpkin:** Float shade on the yellow rainbow stripe.
20. **Medium Flesh:** Paint the cat's nose.
21. **Tompte Red:** Paint the lips on all the fish. Paint the "No Fishing" sign, lines on the reel, and the fishing pole (1/8" dowel).
22. **Kim Gold:** Paint all the stars and dots on the clouds, and the halo on the cat. Line the cat's wings and paint the edging on the cat's wings.
23. **Hauser Dark Green:** Dot the spots on all the fish.
24. **White:** Paint the eyes on all the fish.
25. **Lining:** Using the Itoya lining pen fill in the words on the "No Fishing" sign. Line and stitch everything (refer to the pattern).
26. **Black:** Paint the words on the large fish ("Cat Heaven"). Paint the tops of the cat's shoes. Dot all lettering. Dot the eyes on all fish and the cat. Dot the mouth on one small fish with an open mouth. Dot the eyes and beak on the bird.
27. **True Blue:** Float shade on the top of the rainbow over the red stripe.
28. **White:** Paint the laces on the shoes. Using a fine line brush, line the star highlights here and there on the rainbow, then dot the centers of the star highlights.
29. **Gluing:** Trace the pattern for the pocket and cuffs onto denim, cut them out and glue them in place on the cat's chest and bottom of the pants. Using wood glue, glue the cat cut outs onto the cloud making sure they are positioned correctly over the wings and tail. Glue the small dowel with the sign into the rainbow, glue the longer dowel for the fishing pole into the reel, glue three fish on the rainbow and glue the legs on the cat. Glue the wing on the bird.
30. **Assemble:** Cut four pieces of 19 gauge wire 8" long. Curl and smash the end of the wire, put it through the front drill hole on the large fish sign ("Cat Heaven"). Pull all the way through, then curl the wire on a brush or pencil. Poke the loose end of the wire through the back of the drill holes in the top of the cloud. Curl and smash this end of the wire to secure it in place. Do the same with all the remaining wires till all of the project is assembled. Then using a glue gun, glue the embroidery floss to the reel, in the center of the pole and at the end of the pole, and then glue the fish on the end of the floss.
31. Using a Krylon Matte Spray 1311, seal all of the project. Let dry. Hammer in the saw tooth hanger on the back of the large fish to hang.

COME AND GET IT

This wood is not available through Provo Craft.

PALETTE:
DELTA CERAMCOAT
White	Ivory	Barn Red	Silver (Gleams)
Medium Flesh	Black	Kim Gold (Gleams)	

DECOART AMERICANA
Victorian Blue	Berry Red	Baby Blue	Ultra Blue Deep
Shading Flesh	Blue Grass Green		

SUPPLIES:
- (1) 8" Metal Cake Pan
- Glue Gun
- Graphite Paper
- Large Permanent Black Marker
- (3) 1-1/4" Long Screws
- Krylon Matte Spray 1311
- (2) Small Blue Feathers
- #10 Shader and 10/0 Liner
- Wood Glue
- Itoya .3 Lining Pen
- Checkerboards Stencil #40-0530
- #6 Fabric dye brush (for stippling)

WOODCUTTING HINTS: The cat is cut from 3/4" wood. The arm and wings are cut from 1/2" wood. The stake is 35" long and 3/4" x 1-1/2" wood with one end cut to a sharp point. The overall finished size is 22-1/2" x 13-1/2".

PAINTING INSTRUCTIONS: Trace the basic pattern onto the wood. Add the details as needed.

1. **White:** Paint the cat's wings, soles and toes on the shoes and the woven part of the net.
2. **Ivory:** Paint the cat's face, tail and hands.
3. **Victorian Blue:** Paint the overalls.
4. **Berry Red:** Paint both of the cat's sleeves.
5. **Barn Red:** Using the medium size checks, stencil the checks on both sleeves.
6. **Baby Blue:** Paint the large pocket and cuffs on the overalls. Stipple highlights on the side pocket.
7. **Ultra Blue Deep:** Using a lining brush, paint the lines on the plaid sleeves. Float shade on the lower out side edges of the overalls, inside of the legs, above the tops of both pockets and then on the outside and inside of the cuffs.
8. **Silver (Gleams):** Paint the handle and the rim on the net.
9. **Bluegrass Green:** Use a liner brush and paint the netting on the net, then fill in the inside of the net. Float shade on the outside edges of the netting.
10. **Shading Flesh:** Paint the cat's ears. Stipple blush on the cat's cheeks.
11. **Medium Flesh:** Paint the cat's nose.
12. **Kim Gold:** Paint the halo. With a liner brush line the criss crosses on the wings and paint the edges.
13. **Lining:** Using a .3 Itoya lining pen, fill in the words on the cat's large pocket ("Come and Get It"), then line and stitch everything else (refer to the pattern).
14. **Black:** Fill in the top part of the cat's shoes, the area behind the net, the area by the tail and dot the eyes. Using the wood end of the paint brush, dot all the lettering on the large pocket. Stipple the spots on the cat's face, hands and tail.
15. **White:** Fill in the shoe laces on the cat's shoes. Using a liner brush, paint fine double lines on the cat's sleeves along the side of the dark blue lines.
16. **Gluing:** Using wood glue, glue the wings and arm in place, making sure the top part of the hand is flat and level (for the pan to sit on). Use a glue gun and glue the feathers by the side pocket to look as if they are in the pocket).
17. Using Krylon Matte Spray 1311, seal all of the cat (several thin coats, letting it dry between each coat.) (This is extremely important and will help prevent weathering.
18. **Assemble:** Make sure all areas are pre-drilled for screws then assemble. Using a large permanent black marker write "Bird Seed" on the cake pan. Position the cake pan on the cat's hand and screw in place (screw will be off center). Using two screws, screw the stake to the back of the cat. Fill the pan with bird seed and place outside to feed the birds.

15

PLANT A KISS

This wood is not available through Provo Craft.

PALETTE:
DELTA CERAMCOAT
Ivory   Toffee   White   Empire Gold
Maple Sugar Tan   Tompte Red   Black

DECOART AMERICANA
Toffee   Salem Blue   Napa Red   Cadmium Yellow
Hauser Dark Green   Victorian Blue

SUPPLIES:
4" Clay Pot
Checkerboards Stencil #41-0530
.1 and .3 Itoya Lining Pens
Graphite Paper
10/0 Liner Brush and #6 Flat Shader
(4) 1/4" x 4 1/2" Torn Fabric Strips (preferably green and blue)
Small Stipple Brush (I prefer Loew Cornell #6 Fabric dye brush)
Wood Glue
Stylus
Krylon Matte Spray 1311
Optional Garden Tools

WOOD CUTTING HINTS: The base is 7" x 4" and is cut from 1-1/2" wood. The seed bag is cut from 3/4" wood. The overall finished size is 5-1/2"x 7".

WOOD PREPARATION: Sand the wood, remove the dust with a tack cloth, seal the wood pieces. Trace basic patterns on all three pieces including the pot. Trace the details as needed later. Paint all sides of the project.

PAINTING INSTRUCTIONS:
1. **Ivory:** Paint the lower part of the pot and sides of the base.
2. **Toffee (Americana):** Paint the seed bag.
3. **Toffee Brown (Delta):** With a #6 shader, float shade on the outside edges of the seed bag.
4. **Salem Blue:** Paint the sky (inside the large heart on the pot).
5. **Napa Red:** Paint the top and inside of the pot, top of the base, front sides of the base, small heart on the seed bag, and heart wings on the butterfly (inside the large heart on the pot).
6. **White:** Fill in the hill (inside the large heart on the pot).
7. **Empire Gold:** Paint the main part of the sun (inside the large heart).
8. **Cadmium Yellow:** Paint the rays on the sun. Dot the butterfly body (inside the large heart).
9. **Maple Sugar Tan:** Using a small stipple brush, stipple highlights on the seed bag. Using the Checkerboards Stencil, stencil small checks on the front sides of the base (over the red areas only). With a liner brush fill in and dot the lettering on top of the pot ("Kisses 10 Cents").
10. **Hauser Dark Green:** With a #6 shader, float shade on top of the hill (inside the large heart). Fill in all the small hearts on the pot. With the liner brush line the hill and fill in and dot the lettering on the front of the base ("Love Grows When You Plant A Kiss").
11. **Victorian Blue:** Using a liner brush, fill in and dot the lettering on the seed bag ("Seeds of Love").
12. **Tompte Red:** Fill in the lips above the large heart on the pot.
13. **Line:** Using a .3 lining pen, apply a solid line around the large heart, round edge of the sun and lips. Apply x's on the front of the base, line the back of the hill and write the word "Smack" by the lips. Using a .1 lining pen, solid line the butterfly and all the small hearts, put x's on the bottom of the seed bag, and x's and o's around the large heart. Fill in the sun's face and add expression lines surrounding the lips. Put running stitches around the rays of the sun, seed bag and the front (Ivory) area of the base. Add texture lines on the highlighted areas of the seed bag. Put stitches on all the small hearts and around the large heart and on the checks on the front side of the base. Apply echo lines around the lettering on the bag, top of the pot, and the base. Write the word, "Love", above the green heart plants on the hill (inside the large heart).
14. **Black:** With a stylus, dot the lettering on the word "Smack", and dot the X's and O's (around the large heart).
15. **Assemble and Glue:** Tie and glue the material scraps onto the 4 corners of the seed bag, then with wood glue, glue the pot and seed bag on the base (seed bag is slightly turned). Let the glue dry.
16. Seal using Krylon Matte Spray 1311. Let dry.

A STITCH IN TIME SAVES 9 LIVES

This wood is not available through Provo Craft.

PALETTE:
DELTA CERAMCOAT
Ivory   White   Maple Sugar Tan   Dolphin Grey
Dusty Mauve   Black   Kim Gold (Gleams)

DECOART AMERICANA
Napa Red   Kelly Green   Cadmium Yellow   Victorian Blue
Hauser Dark Green

SUPPLIES:
Krylon Matte Spray 1311
.3 Itoya Lining Pen
Small Wood Heart 1/2"x 1/8"
(8) Assorted Color Hat Pins
Needle and Thread
Fabric Scrap for Basket
Dowels 1/8" (2" long) 1/4" (9" long)
Loew Cornell #6 Fabric Dye Brush for stippling
(7) Small Spools of Thread (in variety of colors)
Material–Red 7" x 3-1/2" , Green 1/2" x 11", Tan 2" x 2-1/2"
Embroidery Floss in 4 Colors–Red, Green, Blue, and Yellow
Small Wicker Basket
Steel Wool
Stylus
Spanish Moss
Glue Gun
Wood Glue
Thimble

Wing pattern is on page 18, all other patterns are on the insert.

WOOD CUTTING HINTS: The cat and base are cut from 3/4" wood. The arm, flower and bird are cut from 1/2" wood. The wings are cut from 1/4" wood. The overall finished size is 10-3/8" x 7".

PAINTING INSTRUCTIONS:
1. **Ivory:** Paint the cat's face, hands and legs.
2. **White:** Paint the wings and the cat's bloomers.
3. **Maple Sugar Tan:** With a stipple brush, stiple the spots on the cat's face, legs and hands.
4. **Hauser Dark Green:** Paint the cat's sleeves.
5. **Dolphin Grey:** Paint the small wooden heart.
6. **Victorian Blue:** Paint the small bird. Using a stylus dot the small wood heart.
7. **Ivory:** Dot the sleeves on the cat using the wood end of a stippling brush.
8. **Napa Red:** Paint the base and the petals on the flower.
9. **Kelly Green:** Paint the leaves and the dowel on the flower.
10. **Dusty Mauve:** Stipple the blush on the cheeks. Fill in the nose and ears. Paint the top of the flower.
11. **Cadmium Yellow:** Paint the bird's beak.
12. **Kim Gold (Gleams):** Paint the basket if desired. Fill in the lines and edges of the wings and the halo on the cat.
13. **Itoya .3 Pen:** Line everything (refer to the pattern). Fill in the lettering on the wings ("A Stitch in time…Saves Nine Lives…").
14. **Black:** Paint the cat's shoes. Dot the cat's and bird's eyes. Fill in the cat's mouth. Dot all the lettering on the wings.
15. **Assemble:** Using wood glue, glue the wings on the cat and the small heart sideways (for wing) on the bird and glue the arm on the cat. With the red fabric lay it so the short ends are on the sides then cut a notch on both top sides 1-1/2" down x 3/4" across as shown on the illustration. With a needle and thread, sew a running stitch along the top side approximately 1/4" from the edge to gather the dress. Do the same with the tan fabric along one 2" side to gather the apron. With the green fabric tie a bow. Using a glue gun, glue the dress, apron and bow onto the cat. Cut a piece of tan fabric 1/2" or larger than the top of the basket all the way around. Fill the basket with steel wool (be careful when handling it can give you metal slivers). Cover the basket with the fabric and tuck in around the edges then glue along the inside of the basket with a glue gun. Roll all four colors of the embroidery floss into balls. Glue the red, blue and green balls onto the fabric on top of the basket and set aside the yellow ball. Place the seven spools of thread on the long dowel. Using a glue gun, glue the Spanish moss around the bottom of the bird to make a nest (making sure not to cover the drill hole in the bottom of the bird). Fill the thimble with glue (this is hot!!! so be careful). Place the flower stem in the glue and tuck in the Spanish moss around the stem. Hold the flower in place till set. Glue the end of the yellow floss under the birds wing, place the bird on top of the long dowel. String the yellow floss back and forth in the cat's hands then glue in place. Glue the yellow ball on the base by the side of the basket.
16. Glue the girl on the back of the base and glue the basket and thimble in place and let dry.
17. Seal using Krylon Matte Spray 1311.

WOOD PREPARATION: Sand the wood, remove the dust with a tack cloth, seal all the wood. The base should have a 1/4" hole drilled at the right back of the base approximately 1" from the edges. Glue a 9" long dowel into the hole using wood glue. Glue a 2" long dowel into the flower.

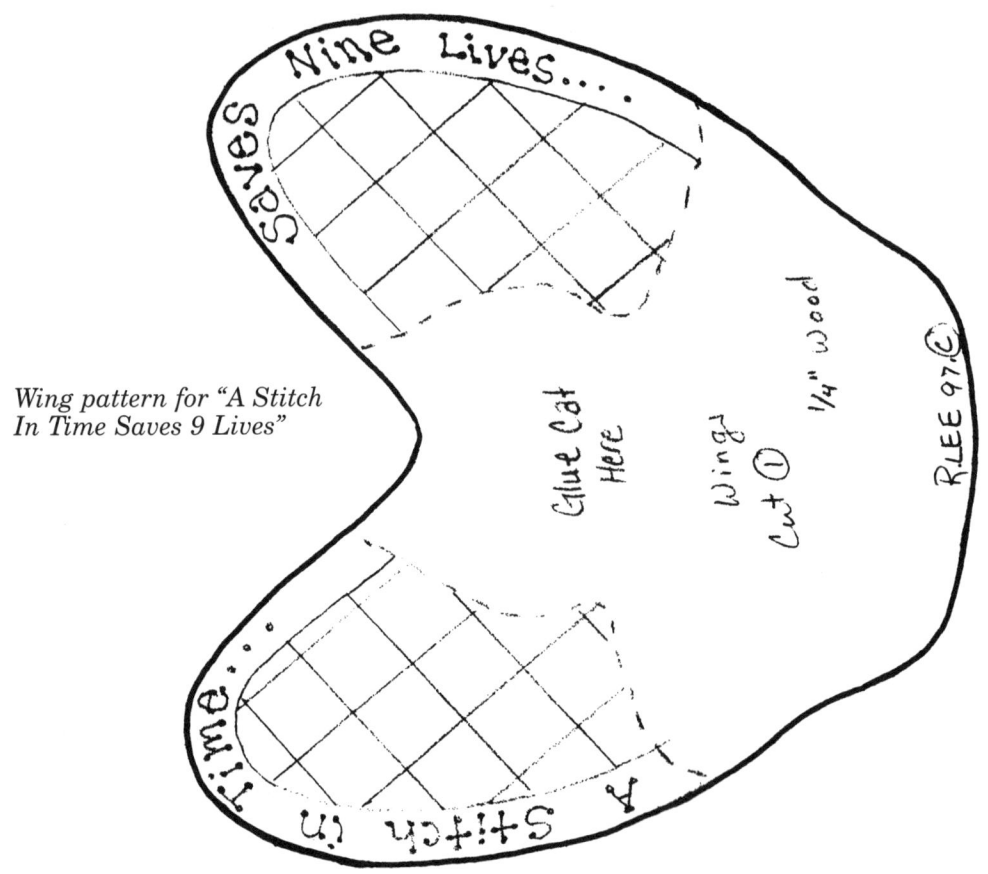

Wing pattern for "A Stitch In Time Saves 9 Lives"

DON'T HIDE YOUR LITE
(Lamp with Tail Switch)

This wood is not available through Provo Craft.

SPECIAL INSTRUCTIONS: This lamp requires some pre-assembly before painting. Please follow all preparation instructions before beginning.

SUPPLIES:

Hacksaw
Glue Gun
Graphite Paper
Wood Glue
Ruler
.5 Itoya Liner Pen
Checkerboards Stencil #41-0530
(1) 4" Plated Steel Nipple Threaded 1/8" IP
(2) Steel Locknuts 1/8" IP Thread
(1) Lamp Socket (with pull chain)
(1) 12" Beaded Chain Extension (w/connector)
(1) Lamp Cord Set (with molded on plug)
1/4" Copper Tubing (cut 3/4" long)
(3) 2" Long Sheet Rock Grabber Screws
(1) Pre-cut 6-1/2" x 11-1/2" Roman Shield Plaque 10-0545 (for base)
Krylon Matte 1311 Sealer
#6 Fabric Brush, #10, 6 and 2 Shader Brushes and 10/0 Liner
Universal Lamp Shade (top 5", bottom 8", height 6-1/4") (any size will work)

WOODCUTTING HINTS: The tail, cat front, center divider and cat back are all cut from 3/4" wood. The large bunch of apples, small bunch of apples and worm are all cut from 1/2" wood. The overall finished size is 12" x 19".

WOOD PREPARATION: Pre-drill only the back of the cat and center divider using a 1/8" drill bit. (Do Not pre-drill the cat front.)

PREPARATION:
1. When tracing and cutting wood for this project, you must be as exact and close to the pattern as possible. This will save a lot of time in adjustment and sanding later. Also pre-drill all the screw holes on the cat back, before assembling.
2. **Sanding:** The tail on this lamp requires heavy sanding to ease movement of the tail switch function.
3. **Pre-assembly of Cat:** The cat must be completely pre-assembled before painting. Be careful when putting the lamp together that the measurements are precise. Screws must be located in the positions marked on the pattern. (These have been carefully measured and placed in certain positions to blend in with the painting design, as well as making the lamp function properly.)
4. After the cat is assembled, sand the entire project well so the assembled edges are smooth. (A thin belt sander is recommended, but sanding can be done with a palm sander or by hand.)

Cat Assembly:
1. Trace, cut, drill and sand all the pieces.
2. Glue the back and center divider together, carefully matching all the edges.
3. Using a ruler, measure 3/4" of the copper tubing (it should say off not on). Cut with a hack saw and sand the rough edges, then insert the copper guard into the pivot screw hole on the tail piece.
4. Insert the 4" plated steel nipple into the 3/8" pre-drilled hole in the raised arm on the center divider. Leave approximately 1/2" of the nipple above the wood. Secure in place using the two steel locknuts. Put one locknut on the inside on the bottom of the nipple and one on the top outside area of the nipple against the wood.
5. **Lamp Socket:** Screw the lamp socket onto the top of the steel nipple, remove the bell end from the pull cord chain and set the bell aside for later.
6. Connect the beaded chain to the pull cord using the connector, then thread the chain through the pull hole in the center divider and then through the drill hole in the tail.
7. **Tail Pivot:** Put a 2" pivot screw in place through the drill hole in the back of the cat. Then with a copper guard inserted in the tail piece, place the copper guard over the pivot screw (the long part of the tail is on the outside of the cat). *Note: The copper guard protects the wood from wearing through at the pivot point.
8. **Adjust Chain:** Position the tail by gently pulling the outside of the tail down. This will raise the inside of the tail to its highest point. Pull the chain (under the tail) so it is snug, then using the bell end that was set aside, secure the bell on the chain under the tail with the bell against the wood.
9. **Test Tail Switch:** To check the tension on the chain, push the outside of the tail toward the cat in an upward motion. It will make a clicking sound each time the tail is lifted if assembled properly. If an adjustment is needed, raise or lower the steel nipple by adjusting the locknuts either up or down. (*Note: Most pull cords require a 1" allowance for the switch function.) If the switch works properly, you can now trim off the excess chain.
10. **Lamp Cord Installation:** To install the lamp cord, disassemble the top portion of the lamp socket. (This comes apart just below the chain opening.) Using the lamp cord set, thread the bare end of the wire through the opening in the bottom of the cat, up through the steel nipple to the light socet. Connect the bare wire ends to the lamp socket according to the package assembly directions. Now reassemble the lamp socket. Then using the glue gun, carefully glue the cord in place against the left side of the wood on the inside of the cat. (This is to keep the cord from interfering with the tail function.) Now insert a light bulb in thelamp socket. Plug in the cord and test the lamp.
11. **Cat Front**: Using 2" screws, place all the screws in the pre-drilled holes in the back of the cat. Place the front of the cat against the center divider, matching all the edges and screw it in place. (This can be glued if desired. I prefer not gluing so it can be removed if repairs are needed.)
12. **Sand:** A final sanding of all edges is needed at this point. I prefer a thin belt sander, but a palm sander can be used or it can be done by hand. Make sure all the edges are even, some tight places will require hand sanding. (Be careful to protect the cord while sanding so it does not become damaged.)
13. Sand, tack and seal as normal.

PALETTE:
DECOART AMERICANA
Calico Red	Victorian Blue	Baby Blue
Ultra Blue Deep	Bright Green	Holly Green
Yellow Light	Shading Flesh	
Gel Stains (Walnut)		

DELTA CERAMCOAT
White	Ivory	Barn Red
Tompte Red	Black Cherry	Medium Flesh
Autumn Brown	Black	Spice tan
Kim Gold (Gleams)		

SUPPLIES:
Fabric Gel Medium

PAINTING INSTRUCTIONS: Paint all sides of the wood.
1. Using graphite paper, trace the patterns onto all sides of the wood. (Side patterns are not given, blend them to match the front and back.)
2. **White:** Paint the toes and soles on the shoes and the cat's wings.
3. **Ivory:** Paint all of the tail. (Lift the tail and wedge a toothpick underneath so the entire tail can be painted.) Paint the face and both of the hands.
4. **Calico Red:** Paint the cat's sleeves.
5. **Victorian Blue:** Paint the cat's overalls.
6. **Barn Red:** Using the Checkerboards Stencil (medium checks), stencil all the sides of the cat's shirt. (The area between the head and wings needs to be hand-painted.)
7. **Baby Blue:** Paint the cuffs on the overalls, the large front pocket and two small pockets on the back of the cat. Stipple the highlights on the apple filled pockets.
8. **Ultra Blue Deep:** Using a #6 shader, float shade on the cuffs, the line between the legs, apple filled pockets and lower sides of the overalls. Using a liner brush paint the plaid lines on the sleeves.
9. **Tompte Red:** Paint all of the apples.
10. **Black Cherry:** Using a #6 shader float shades on all of the apples.
11. **White:** Float the highlights on all of the apples, then with a liner brush paint fine double lines on the plaid shirt.
12. **Bright Green:** Paint the worm and leaves on the apples.
13. **Holly Green:** Using a #2 shader brush, float shade on all the leaves and the worm.
14. **Yellow Light:** Paint the highlights on the worm's chest and head and on the leaves.
15. **Shading Flesh:** Stipple the cat's cheeks and fill in his ears.
16. **Medium Flesh:** Paint the cat's nose.
17. **Autumn Brown:** Paint the stems on the apples.
18. **Kim Gold Gleams:** Paint the cat's halo, then line criss-crosses on the wings and base the wing edges. Dot the rivets on the cat's back pockets.
19. **.5 Itoya Pen:** Fill in all the words on the cat's large pocket. ("Don't Hide Your Lite!"). Line everything else (refer to the pattern).
20. **Black:** Paint the cat's shoes. Dot the eyes on the cat and worm. Dot all the lettering. Stipple the spots on the cat's tail, face and hands.
21. **White:** Paint the laces on the cat's shoes.
22. **Spice Tan:** Paint all of the lamp shade. Next, using a ruler and pencil, find the back seam on the lamp shade, on the bottom and top edges make a mark directly across from the seam. Now make a mark vertically across from each other evenly spaced between the other marks so you have four even sections. Measure and mark again evenly between existing marks. You should end up with 8 equal spaces, as shown in the illustration. Next divide all these spaces in half again to end up with 16 spaces. (These are reference points only.) You will need these on the top and bottom of the shade. Now turning the shade with the bottom of the shade on the table measure 1-1/4" from top and bottom on the sides of the shade. Do this all the way around the shade marking lightly with a pencil. Draw a line connecting these marks all the way around the top and bottom of the sides on the shade (see illustration). Using the reference points and ruler draw 16 vertical lines around the shade, then draw a half circle on the top and bottom bands.
23. **Autumn Brown:** Mix 1/2 paint and 1/2 Fabric Gel Medium, then with a #10 shader, shade along the top and bottom bands and the 16 vertical lines. Shade along the half circles.
24. **.5 Itoya Pen:** Line along the shaded areas and line the bold drawn lines. *(instructions continue on page 22)*

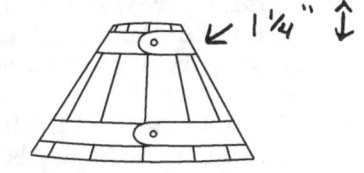

25. **Black:** Make nail dots in the center of both half circles.
26. **Walnut Gel Stain:** Stain the base using the wipe on and wipe off method. Let dry.
27. Using wood glue, glue the cat, apples and worm in place on the base.
28. Using Krylon Matte Spray 1311, seal the entire project. Let dry.

MOM'S HALO

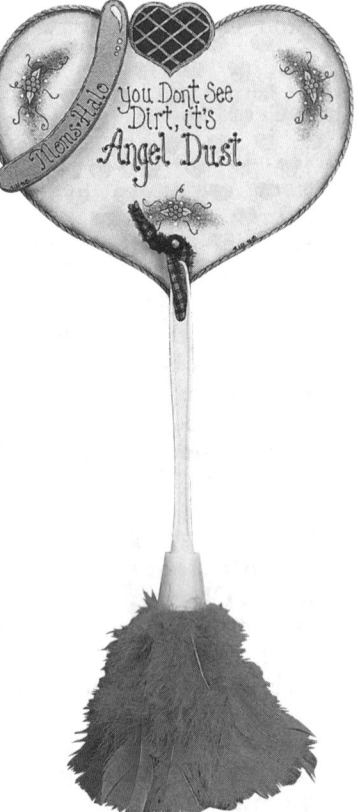

This wood is not available through Provo Craft.

PALETTE:

DELTA CERAMCOAT
Western Sunset	Village Green	Black
Dolphin Grey	Kim Gold	White

DECOART AMERICANA
Cranberry Wine	Napa Red	Sand
Hauser Dark Green		

SUPPLIES:

(1) 1" Wood Peg	.1 and .5 Itoya Permanent Lining Pen
Wood Glue	Krylon Matte Spray 1311
(1) Sawtooth Hanger	Feather Duster
Fabric Scrap 1/2" x 12"	Sweethearts Stencil #41-0527
#10 Shader and 10/0 Liner	#6 Fabric Dye Brush (for stippling)
White Graphite Paper (for tracing the pattern)	

WOODCUTTING HINTS: The large heart is cut from 3/4" wood. The halo is cut from 1/2" wood. The overall finished size is 9-1/2" x 7-1/2".

PAINTING INSTRUCTIONS:
1. **Sand:** Paint the heart.
2. **Western Sunset:** Using the large hearts on the Sweetheart stencil, stencil the hearts on the large wooden heart.
3. **Cranberry Wine:** With a #10 shader, float shade around the edges of the large heart.
4. **Napa Red:** Trace on the pattern using graphite paper. Fill in the small red heart on the top center of the project. Paint the peg.
5. **Hauser Dark Green:** Stipple the greenery on each side and bottom of the large heart.
6. **Village Green:** Paint the leaves on the small flowers over the greenery.
7. **Dolphin Grey:** Dot the flowers on the greenery.
8. **Kim Gold:** Paint the halo and fill in the edges on both the large and small hearts. Then with a 10/0 liner brush, paint the criss-cross lines on the small heart and dot the center on the flowers and the center of the peg.
9. **White:** Dot around the flowers on the greenery and fill in the highlights on the halo.
10. **Lining:** Trace the words onto the large heart ("You don't see dirt, it's Angel Dust"). Trace the words on the halo ("Mom's Halo"). Using a .5 Itoya lining pen, write the words on both pieces. Line the vines on the greenery. Using a .1 Itoya pen line echo lines on the words "Angel Dust". Fill in the rope edging around the large heart. Outline the small flowers and leaves on the greenery. Dot dash around the edges of the small heart.
11. **Black:** Dot all the lettering.
12. Using wood glue, glue the halo and peg in place.
13. Using Krylon Matte Spray 1311, spray the entire heart and let it dry.
14. Duster: Using fabric scraps tie the fabric in the handle on the duster, for the hanger. Next attach the saw tooth hanger on the back of the project.

ENDURE TO THE END

This wood is not available through Provo Craft.

PALETTE:
DELTA CERAMCOAT

White	Ivory	Jubilee Green
Mocha	Maple Sugar Tan	Autumn Brown
Medium Flesh	Dusty Mauve	Kim Gold
Black	Spice Tan	

DECO ART AMERICANA

Mint Julep Green	Holly Green	Yellow Green
Hauser Dark Green	True Ochre	Berry Red
Orchid	Victorian Blue	Baby Blue
Yellow Light	Napa Red	Spice Pink
Bright Green	Shading Flesh	Leaf Green

SUPPLIES:

Wood Glue	Glue Gun	Itoya .3 Lining Pen	Grey Graphite
(8) 1-1/2" Screws	Tan Fabric Torn 2" x 2-1/2"	Needle and Thread	Red Fabric Torn 3" x 5"
Krylon Matte Spray 1311	#6 Fabric Brush	#2, 6, & 10 Shaders	10/0 Liner
(4) 1-1/4" Screws (sheet rock grabber screws)		Checkerboards Stencil #41-0530 (small)	

WOODCUTTING HINTS: The two mountain backs, two bases, boy cat and girl cat are cut from 3/4" wood. The girl cat's arm, boy cat's arm, both inner pieces, rose vine birdhouse, grasshopper, fishing pole, frog and tree are all cut from 1/2" wood. The overall finished size of each piece is 8-1/4" x 7-3/4".

PAINTING INSTRUCTIONS:
1. Trace all the basic patterns on the wood pieces.
2. **Mint Julep Green:** Paint the hills on the inner girls and inner boy's side pieces.
3. **White:** Paint the wings on both cats. Paint the clouds, snow caps on the mountains, background on the fishing pole and rose vine, girl's bloomers, fence on the girl's side and toe and soles on the boy's shoes. Paint the frog's eyes.
4. **Ivory:** Paint the faces and hands on both of the cats. Paint the gir'ls legs and the boy's tail.
5. **Holly Green:** Paint the area under the snow caps on the mountains, then with a #10 shader float shade on the hills on both the inner side pieces.
6. **Jubilee Green:** Paint the frog and grasshopper.

7. **Yellow Green:** Stipple highlights on the frog's knees, and feet, and mouth. Stipple the highlights on the grasshopper's head and paint the grasshopper's back leg.
8. **True Ochre:** Paint the outside edges on both suns. Paint the grasshopper's back shin.
9. **Mocha:** Paint the old fence posts on the boys side. Paint the tree trunk.
10. **Hauser Dark Green:** Dab the top of the frog's knees and paint the area between the frog's front legs. Base the tree and the girl's sleeve.
11. **Maple Sugar Tan:** Stipple the spots on the girl cat's face, hands and legs. Paint the fishing creel and the tops on the old fence posts and dot the girl's sleeve.
12. **Spice Tan:** With a #2 shader float highlights on the left side of the old fence posts. Stipple the highlights on the center of the tree trunk. Paint the reel on the fishing pole.
13. **Autumn Brown:** Paint both bases. Shade the edges of the tree trunk. Shade the right side of the old fence posts. Float the inside edges of the creel. Paint the edges on the lid of the creel.
14. **Berry Red:** Paint the three petal flower on the girl's inner side. Paint the lady bug on the old fence post. Paint the fishing pole and lower half of the fishing bobber. Paint the boy cat's sleeve.
15. **Orchid:** Paint the star shaped flower on the girl's inner side. Dot all the wildflowers at the base of the old fence post. Stipple shades on the clouds. With a #2 shader, shade the cheeks on the clouds.
16. **Victorian Blue:** Paint the boy cat's overalls.
17. **Baby Blue:** Paint the birdhouse. Stipple the shade on the clouds. Paint the boy cat's pocket and cuffs. Then with a #2 shader, float the areas behind the eyes on both clouds. Fill in the mouths on the clouds.
18. **Yellow Light:** With a #2 shader, paint the highlights on the grasshopper wing, feet and smile. Fill in the heart the grass hopper is holding. Paint both suns and line the rays on the edges of the suns. Dot or paint the centers of all the flowers.
19. **Napa Red:** Paint the roof and pole on the birdhouse. Using the Checkerboards Stencil stipple the small checks on the boy cat's arm.
20. **Victorian Blue:** Paint the plaid lines on the boy's sleeve.
21. **Spice Pink:** Paint the roses on the rose vine. Fill in the girl cat's mouth. Stipple the blush on the girl's cheeks.
22. **Bright Green:** Stipple the highlights on the mountains. Dot the leaves on the rose vine. Paint the stems on the flowers (girl's inner side).
23. **Medium Flesh:** Paint the boy cat's nose.
24. **Shading Flesh:** Stipple the boy cat's cheeks and fill in his ears.
25. **Dusty Mauve:** Fill in the girl cat's nose and ears.
26. **Leaf Green:** Stipple the highlights on the pine tree and paint the leaves and stems on the wild flowers. Paint the leaves on the flowers on the girl's inner side.
27. **Kim Gold (Gleams):** Paint the halos on both cats. Line their wings and paint the edges on both cat's wings.
28. **Black:** Paint the top of the boy cat's shoes and fill in the lady bug's face and feet. Make heart spots on the back of the lady bug. Fill in the eyes on the clouds. Dot the hole on the birdhouse and eyes on both cats, frog and grasshopper. Stipple the spots on the boy cat face, hand and tail. Fill in the area by the boy cat's tail. Paint the girl's shoes. Fill in the dark areas on the grasshopper. Float shade on the overalls.
29. **White:** Using a liner paint the face on the lady bug and highlight on its feet. Dot the eyes on the grasshopper. Paint highlights on the grasshopper's tail and feet. Fill in the eyes on the sun (girl's side). Paint the shoe laces on the boy cat and paint fine double lines on his sleeve.
30. **Black:** Fill in the pupils on the sun on the girl's side.
31. **Lining:** Using a .3 Itoya lining pen, fill in the words on the girl's wings ("Endure to the end...Be it Foe or Friend"). Line and stitch everything else by referring to the pattern.
32. **Assemble:** Mark and pre-drill screw holes on the back of the mountain and inner side pieces. Using 1-1/4" screws, screw the inner side piece to the front of the mountain as shown. Using 1-1/2" screws, pre-drill the base and attach the base to the mountain back and inner side piece. (You may also glue these in addition to screwing to add more support.) Next, using red fabric and needle and thread, gather one long edge of the red fabric and fit it to the girl's neck. Glue in place using a glue gun. Gather the tan fabric in the same way along one short edge to make the girl's apron. Glue at the girl's neck (make sure to allow room for the girl's arm later).
33. **Gluing:** Using wood glue, glue the boy cat in the corner next to the mountain and inner boy's side (make sure his toe is right in the corner). Next glue his arm in place, glue the tree on the base at the edge of the mountains, and glue the fishing pole and creel on the base. Also, glue the frog on the front of the base by the old fence post. Next glue the girl with her back to the inner side piece (girl side), her foot against the fence and her wings against the cloud. Glue her arm in place over the dress. Make sure her hand is flat against the fence. Glue the rose vine on the base at the edge of the mountains. Glue the grasshopper on the base, further in the front towards the center of the base.
34. **Spray Seal:** Using Krylon matte spray 1311, seal both finished pieces and let dry.

SUNSHINE QUILT

This wood is not available through Provo Craft.

PALETTE:
DELTA CERAMCOAT
Queen Anne's Lace
Dolphin Grey
Autumn Brown
Black

Barn Red
Nightfall
Western Sunset

Maple Sugar Tan
Spice Tan
Empire Gold

DECO ART AMERICANA
Hauser Dark Green   Dark Chocolate

SUPPLIES:
Wood Glue
Krylon Matte Spray 1311
#6 Shader
Itoya .5 Lining Pen
19 Gauge Wire-18"
(2) 1/2" Wood Spools
(4) 1/2" Wood Buttons
(4) Small" Primitive Wood Stars
(4) 7" Long Strands Red Embroidery Floss
(4) 5/8" x 5/8" Green Checked Fabric Scraps
(4) 5/8" x 5/8" Red and Tan Checked Fabric Scraps and Red Fabric 1/2" x 1-1/2" (for spools)

WOODCUTTING HINTS: The piece is cut from 3/4" wood. The overall finished size is 10" x 6".

PAINTING INSTRUCTIONS:
1. **Queen Anne's Lace:** Paint the center of the quilt.
2. **Hauser Dark Green:** Paint the corner patches.
3. **Barn Red:** Paint the outer edge center patches.
4. **Maple Sugar Tan:** Paint the patches on the right side of each red patch.
5. **Dolphin Grey:** Paint the remaining patches.
6. **Nightfall:** Shade the edges on all blue patches.
7. **Spice Tan:** Shade all the inside edges on the center area of the quilt (where the writing goes).
8. **Autumn Brown:** Shade the edges on the tan patches.
9. **Dark Chocolate:** Shade the edges on the red patches.
10. **Western Sunset:** Dot the blue patches.
11. **Empire Gold:** Paint the four small wooden stars.
12. **Itoya .5 Pen:** Line the words on the center of the quilt.
13. **Black:** Shade the edges on all the green squares. Dot all the lettering.
14. Glue the red fabric pieces on the Barn Red patches. Glue the green fabric pieces on the dark green corner patches (make sure not to cover over the drilled holes). Glue the red fabric on the wooden spools. Thread embroidery floss through the center holes on the four buttons and tie into bows. Glue the stars on the tan patches and the buttons on the green corner patches.
15. **Itoya Pen:** Apply the stitching and single stitches on everything.
16. **Assemble:** Cut an 18" piece of wire. Loosely curl the center part of the wire. Thread the spools onto the wire, and poke the ends of the wire through the back of the drill holes leaving approximately 2" of wire through the front of the drill hole. Curl the ends of the wire on the paint brush (wood end) or on a pencil.
17. Using Krylon Matte Spray, seal the entire project and let dry.

GUARDIAN KITTY 11-2179
(PLANT STAKE)

PALETTE:

DELTA CERAMCOAT
White
Maple Sugar Tan
Dusty Mauve
Black
Kim Gold (Gleams)

DECOART AMERICANA
Sand
Hauser Dark Green
Buttermilk

SUPPLIES:

5/16" Dowel (12" long)
Needle
Red Fabric Torn 9" x 5"
Krylon Matte Spray 1311
Wood Glue
Green Fabric Torn 3/4" x 11"
#6 Shader

19 Gauge Wire (5" long)
Thread
Tan Fabric Torn 3" x 4"
Stylus
Glue Gun
10/0 Liner
Itoya .5 Lining Pen

WOODCUTTING HINTS: The cat is cut from 3/4" wood. The arm and wings are cut from 3/8" wood. The overall finished size is 17" x 10".

PAINTING INSTRUCTIONS:

1. **White:** Paint the cat's wings.
2. **Sand:** Paint the cat's legs, face and hands.
3. **Hauser Dark Green:** Paint the cat's sleeves and the 12" dowel.
4. **Buttermilk:** Paint the cat's bloomers. Using a stylus make dots on the cat's sleeves.
5. **Maple Sugar Tan:** Stipple the spots on the cat's face, hands and legs.
6. **Dusty Mauve:** Stipple the blush on the cat's cheeks. Dot the nose. Fill in the cat's ears.
7. **Kim Gold:** Paint the halo and edges on the wings. Using a 10/0 liner brush, paint the criss-crosses on the cat's wings.
8. **Itoya .5:** Fill in the lettering on the wings ("Love Bears all Things") and ("XOX Kisses and hugs...Are Patches of Love!!!"). Fill in the cat's face and line everything (refer to the pattern).
9. **Black:** Paint the cat's shoes. Dot the cat's eye and all the lettering.
10. **Dress:** Using a needle and thread and red fabric, gather one 9" side to make the dress. (Adjust to fit the cat's neck.) With the tan fabric gather one 3" edge to make the apron. Tie the green fabric into a bow.
11. **Assemble:** Using a glue gun, glue the dress and apron on the cat so the gathers match at the cat's neck. Glue the green bow over the stitching. With a 5" long piece of 19 gauge wire, poke the wire through the drilled hole in the back of the wings then through the back of the cat's body, through the dress and through the back of the cat's arm. Secure the wire by curling on a pencil or paint brush and smashing the wire flat on the front and back of the cat. Using wood glue, glue the dowel in the drill hole under the cat's tummy.
12. **Sealer:** Using Krylon Matte Spray, seal the project and let dry.

Put in your favorite plant.